DATE DUE

		PRINTED IN U.S.A.

THEODORE ROOSEVELT

OUR TWENTY-SIXTH PRESIDENT

by Ann Graham Gaines

THE CHILD'S WORLD®

PUBLISHED IN THE UNITED STATES OF AMERICA

THE CHILD'S WORLD®
1980 Lookout Drive • Mankato, MN 56003-1705
800-599-READ • www.childsworld.com

ACKNOWLEDGMENTS
The Child's World®: Mary Berendes, Publishing Director

The Creative Spark: Mary McGavic, Project Director; Shari Joffe, Editorial
Director; Deborah Goodsite, Photo Research; Nancy Ratkiewich, Page Production

The Design Lab: Kathleen Petelinsek, Design

Content Adviser: Stacy A. Cordery, Professor of History, Monmouth College,
Monmouth, Illinois

PHOTOS
Cover and page 3: National Portrait Gallery, Smithsonian Institution/Art
Resource, NY (detail); National Portrait Gallery, Smithsonian Institution/Art
Resource, NY

Interior: The Art Archive: 16, 34 (Culver Picture); Art Resource, NY: 20 (Snark);
Associated Press Images: 10, 12; Corbis: 6 and 38 (Gail Mooney), 15 and 39
(Steve Kaufman), 19 and 38, 35 (Bettmann); The Granger Collection, New
York: 13, 21, 23, 24, 25, 28, 33 and 39; The Image Works: 29 (Roger-Viollet),
32 (ARPL/HIP); iStockphoto: 44 (Tim Fan), 36 (Bonnie Jacobs); Library of
Congress: 14 (Manuscript Division, Papers of Theodore Roosevelt); National
Park Service, Manhattan Sites, New York, NY: 5; National Park Service, Sagamore
Hill National Historic Site: 9; North Wind Picture Archives: 27, 31; Photo
Researchers, Inc.: 37 (Science Source); Theodore Roosevelt Association: 8 (used
with the permission of the Houghton Library, Harvard University (bMS Am 1541
(288, no. 2))); Theodore Roosevelt Collection, Harvard College Library: 4, 7, 11,
18, 26, 30; U.S. Air Force photo: 45; White House Historical Association (White
House Collection) (detail): 17.

LIBRARY OF CONGRESS CATALOGING-IN-PUBLICATION DATA
Gaines, Ann.
  Theodore Roosevelt / by Ann Graham Gaines.
      p. cm.— (Presidents of the U.S.A.)
  Includes bibliographical references and index.
  ISBN 978-1-60253-054-6 (library bound : alk. paper)
  1. Roosevelt, Theodore, 1858–1919—Juvenile literature. 2. Presidents—United
States—Biography—Juvenile literature. I. Title. II. Series.

E757.G245 2008
973.91'1092—dc22
  [B]
                                                        2008004367

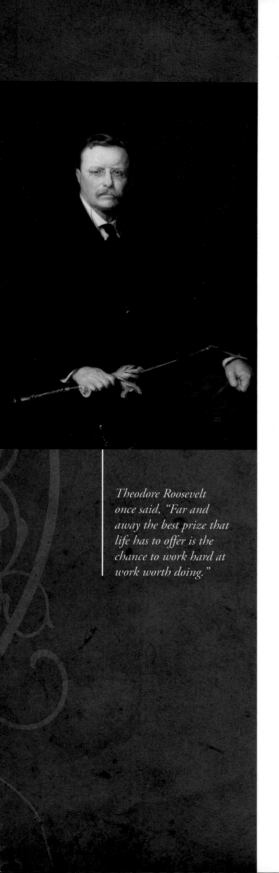

Theodore Roosevelt once said, "Far and away the best prize that life has to offer is the chance to work hard at work worth doing."

TABLE OF CONTENTS

CHAPTER ONE

YOUNG ROOSEVELT

Today Theodore Roosevelt is remembered mainly because he was the twenty-sixth president of the United States. People are impressed by the fact that he was the youngest president ever, taking office at age 42. **Politics** was indeed a huge part of Theodore Roosevelt's life. When he became president, he had already held several other political offices. But he was interested in many other things besides politics. He also gained fame as a soldier, author, and outdoorsman. He traveled all over the American West, down the Amazon River, and into the wilds of Kenya.

Theodore Roosevelt fought health problems as a young child, but he grew up to become an active, energetic man who worked hard at everything he did.

Theodore Roosevelt did not start out his life in the wilderness. He was born on October 27, 1858, in New York City. His family was wealthy and lived in a mansion. Theodore Roosevelt Sr. was an important businessman. The

Theodore Roosevelt admired his mother (left) a great deal. "My mother, Martha Bulloch, was a sweet, gracious, beautiful southern woman, a delightful companion and beloved to everybody," he wrote.

In 1865, when he was still a little boy, Theodore Roosevelt watched Abraham Lincoln's funeral procession pass by his grandfather's house in New York City.

Roosevelts had four children: Anna, Theodore, Elliot, and Corinne.

As a boy, Theodore Roosevelt may have been spoiled. His parents adored their children. They liked to spend time reading to them and gave them many presents. But the future president's life was not easy. Throughout his childhood, he suffered from asthma. This disease makes it difficult for people to breathe. Night after night, Theodore could not sleep because of his breathing problems. His parents stayed by his side, trying to comfort him when he gasped for

As a boy, Theodore Roosevelt especially liked to read adventure books, both fact and fiction. He enjoyed the reports of explorers, as well as classic tales such as *Robinson Crusoe.*

Roosevelt was born in a beautiful New York City brownstone home. Today, visitors can tour a copy of the building. It includes many original furnishings from the Roosevelt home.

breath. Sometimes Theodore's father put Theodore in their horse-drawn carriage and drove up and down the dark streets of New York for hours. He hoped fresh air would help his son breathe more easily.

The Roosevelt children did not attend public school. Like other rich children of the day, they had **tutors** come to their house to teach them. Their parents also taught them some subjects, including foreign languages. The children were smart. They excelled in history, math, and science.

As a child, Theodore Roosevelt enjoyed indoor activities, such as reading and drawing. But by the time he was 11, he had decided he did not want just a quiet life. When he was young, he was small in size. Once, his father told him, "Theodore, you have the mind, but you do not have the body. You must make your body." After that, the boy worked to make himself strong. To reach his goal, he exercised as much as possible, running, jumping, and playing outside. At age 11, he started to lift weights. He took boxing lessons.

Theodore Roosevelt's parents disagreed about the Civil War. His father supported the Union. His mother, however, was from the South. Members of her family fought for the **Confederacy**.

The Roosevelt family spent their summers in the country. Theodore recalled that he and his brother and sisters looked forward to these trips all year. This photo shows Theodore (standing at left), his brother Elliot, his sister Corinne (seated at left), and a family friend named Edith Carow. Edith would later become Roosevelt's second wife.

In the fall of 1871, 13-year-old Theodore Roosevelt donated several scientific specimens to the American Museum of Natural History. They included the skull of a red squirrel, a turtle shell, and four bird's eggs.

In 1873, Theodore Roosevelt, his brother Elliot, and their sister Corinne lived with a family in Germany in order to learn the German language.

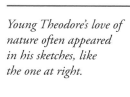

Young Theodore's love of nature often appeared in his sketches, like the one at right.

Theodore Roosevelt Sr. encouraged his son to spend time outside, believing it would help the boy's lungs. Theodore especially liked visiting the second house his family owned in the country. There he roamed the woods. He made collections of the things he gathered there—bugs, rocks, leaves, bones, and nests. He sketched birds and other animals. When Theodore was 13, his father gave him a gun. Poor eyesight made it difficult for him to hit a target. Theodore went to an eye doctor, who gave him glasses. After that, Theodore became an excellent hunter. He enjoyed this activity throughout his life.

The Roosevelts often traveled to their house in the country. They also went to more exotic places. They traveled throughout Europe and in the Middle East. In Egypt, Theodore was fascinated by the pyramids and other ancient ruins. He also greatly enjoyed hunting birds and small mammals.

THEODORE ROOSEVELT SR.

Theodore Roosevelt admired his father all his life. Theodore
Roosevelt Sr. was a successful businessman who made a
fortune from the glass company his father had founded. Unlike
some rich children, Theodore Roosevelt grew up knowing
his father well. Theodore Roosevelt Sr. liked to spend time
with his children. He had other admirable qualities as well.
He was a philanthropist, which means that he gave much
of his money away, helping others. Theodore Sr. donated a
tremendous amount of time and money to charities, such
as hospitals for poor people. He was also a reformer. This
meant he wanted to clean up the government. He and
other powerful men formed a group dedicated to removing
dishonest New York government officials from their jobs.

　　For years, these officials had been accepting bribes.
To get elected, some had paid people to cast extra votes.
Theodore Sr.'s reform group tried to change this. In addition,
he was one of the founders of the Metropolitan Museum of
Art and the American Museum of Natural History, both of
which would become among the world's finest museums.

CHAPTER TWO

POLITICIAN AND FAMILY MAN

In 1876, Theodore went to college. He attended Harvard College in Cambridge, Massachusetts. By this time he was 17 and had reached his full height of five feet eight inches (173 cm) tall. He remained thin, but he had grown strong, thanks to his exercise program. As a boy, Theodore Roosevelt had known few children outside of his family. At college, he was happy to make many new friends. He found time to join many clubs and play sports. He rowed and boxed and ice-skated.

While he was in college, Theodore Roosevelt studied many different subjects. For a long time, he planned to become a naturalist after he finished school. A naturalist is a scientist who studies nature. But over time, he changed his mind. The science professors at Harvard were different from him.

By the time Theodore was 17, he was strong and healthy. He enjoyed hiking, boxing, and lifting weights.

The Roosevelt brothers posed for this photograph during their 1880 hunting trip out west. Theodore is shown on the right.

They did not want to go out into the woods to find specimens. Instead, they insisted their students learn about nature in a laboratory, looking at slides under a microscope. Theodore decided he didn't want to do that. He decided to become a lawyer instead.

Theodore Roosevelt graduated from Harvard in June of 1880. By this time, he had become engaged to Alice Lee, a young woman from a wealthy Boston family. Late that summer, they parted for a time. Roosevelt and his brother traveled by train as far as the Dakota **Territory.** They went there to hike and hunt. In the fall, Roosevelt returned to New York. He and Alice got married in October. After the wedding,

11

Roosevelt was quite taken with beautiful Alice Lee, a 17-year-old from Boston. At first, she did not return his feelings, but she finally agreed to marry him. "After much pleading my own sweet pretty darling consented to be my wife," he wrote. "The aim of my whole life will be to make her happy." Here they are shown in 1880, the year they married.

Roosevelt started law school at Columbia University. But he never became a lawyer. In 1881, he chose to become a **politician** instead when he was asked to run for a seat in the New York State Assembly, part of the state **legislature.**

As a lawmaker, Roosevelt fought for reform. Newspapers and politicians praised Roosevelt for being able to get things done. He insisted that New York's local and state government officials do their jobs well. He wanted the government to give positions to qualified people only. He also made officials explain how they spent the government's money.

Roosevelt was happy being a politician. He also felt happy at home. He and Alice were very much in love. She went with him when he went to assembly meetings in Albany, the capital of New York. When the assembly was not in session, they lived in a house in New York City. Their life there was exciting. They went to parties, plays, and concerts. But Roosevelt continued to dream of spending time in the wilderness. In the summer of 1883, he took a second trip west. He went to what is now North Dakota and bought some land there.

That fall, Roosevelt started his third **term** in the assembly. He spent most weekdays in Albany.

At age 23, Roosevelt was the youngest person ever elected to the New York State Assembly.

In 1883, Roosevelt was named the leader of the **Republican** members of the assembly. He was just 24 years old.

As a lawmaker in the New York State Assembly, Roosevelt worked with Governor Grover Cleveland. Together the two men worked to stamp out **corruption** *in the state's government. Cleveland was elected president in 1884 and again in 1892.*

In 1882, Theodore Roosevelt published his first book, a history of the navy.

Now Alice stayed at home in New York City. She was expecting their first child. In those days, doctors discouraged expectant mothers from traveling or being active. In February of 1884, Alice gave birth to a baby girl. Roosevelt was in Albany. He rushed home when he received the telegram giving him the news. When he arrived, he learned that both his wife and his mother were very ill. They died the next day, just a few hours apart. Theodore Roosevelt was **devastated.** Always a man who enjoyed spending time with his family, he had lost the two people he loved most in the world.

After his wife and mother died, Roosevelt's life changed. To help ease his grief, he returned to work right away. He left his daughter, Alice, with his sister and went back to Albany. But he stayed there for only a few months before heading back to North Dakota. There he started two cattle ranches. He spent time

Theodore Roosevelt was devastated after he lost both his wife and his mother on the same day. This is his journal entry for February 14, 1884—the day the two women died.

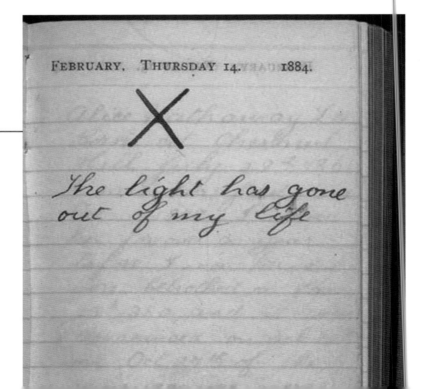

FEBRUARY, THURSDAY 14. 1884.

The light has gone out of my life

Roosevelt dealt with his tragic loss by retreating to the wilds of North Dakota. This photograph shows the inside of his cabin in North Dakota, now part of Theodore Roosevelt National Park.

outdoors. He loved to ride horses. He saddled up to drive cattle and check his fences. On foot, he hunted, fished, and looked for wild foods. Sometimes he got into fistfights. He became even stronger and healthier. For the rest of his life, Roosevelt often talked about his belief in the **"strenuous** life." He urged other people to exercise and improve their health so they could accomplish more in life.

In 1886, Roosevelt ran for mayor of New York City but lost the election.

COWBOYS

In Theodore Roosevelt's day, cowboys captured the imagination of Americans. As railroads were built across the West in the 1860s and 1870s, ranchers began to raise huge herds of cattle. They hired cowboys to tend them.

On the ranches, cowboys "rode the line," checking to make sure there were no holes in the fences. Every year, they went on cattle drives, moving herds of hundreds or even thousands of cattle to stockyards in Kansas and Nebraska. Cowboys from southern Texas had to ride as far as 1,000 miles (1,609 km) to reach their destination. Sometimes along the way, cattle thieves attacked them.

Theodore Roosevelt grew up hearing stories of the exciting cowboy life. In the 1880s, cattle became big business in Montana and the Dakota Territory. After he bought his own ranches, Roosevelt went out with his cowboys to tend his herds, riding a horse equipped with a fine saddle. With spurs on his boots and a revolver at his hip, Roosevelt spent hours outdoors. He loved what he described as a life of freedom and action.

Theodore Roosevelt in the Dakota Territory in the 1880s

CHAPTER THREE

A WAR HERO

In late 1885, a severe winter storm wiped out Theodore Roosevelt's herd of cattle. Rather than start again, Roosevelt decided the time had come for him to return to his old life in New York. He proposed to Edith Carow, a friend of his since childhood. He and Edith left for Europe and married in London in December of 1886. After their return to the United States, the couple lived in their mansion in New York City and in a new country house Roosevelt had built called Sagamore Hill.

In New York, Roosevelt reentered politics. He ran for election as mayor of New York City, in 1886, but lost. In 1888, President Benjamin Harrison asked him to be the nation's civil service commissioner. This put Roosevelt in charge of the federal government's many office

Theodore Roosevelt's second wife, Edith Carow, had been a childhood friend.

Roosevelt enjoyed his years as assistant secretary of the U.S. Navy. "I am having immense fun running the navy," he wrote to a friend.

workers. After that, Roosevelt became New York City's police commissioner, overseeing the police department. Then he became assistant secretary of the U.S. Navy. He helped manage the navy's operations, deciding where to send the nation's ships and sailors. One thing he did was prepare for war. The United States and Spain were on the verge of war, preparing to fight over Cuba and other Spanish colonies.

In 1898, the Spanish-American War began. Roosevelt resigned from his navy job and joined the army. He believed so strongly that Cuba deserved independence from Spain that he asked the army to let him **recruit** his own **regiment.** When he was given permission, he formed the Rough Riders. This unit of

Colonel Theodore Roosevelt is shown at camp during the Spanish-American War in 1898.

THE ROUGH RIDERS

In 1895, the island nation of Cuba began its fight for independence from Spain. At first, the U.S. government did not support the Cubans. But this would change. On February 15, 1898, a U.S. battleship, the *Maine,* exploded in the harbor at Havana. The ship had been sent to the city to protect Americans living there. More than 260 U.S. sailors on the *Maine* were killed, and Americans believed the Spanish were responsible. In April, the United States declared war on Spain. Congress authorized the American military to drive the Spanish out of Cuba. Theodore Roosevelt believed wholeheartedly that the United States was right to enter the Spanish-American War. In fact, he volunteered to go to Cuba and even recruited a group of volunteers. He chose young, fit men who were ready for battle. Some were millionaire outdoorsmen. Others were college football players or cowboys from the West. All the Rough Riders, as Roosevelt's men became known, were tough, courageous men.

Roosevelt and his Rough Riders were among the first U.S. troops to arrive in Cuba, and they achieved great fame. On July 1, 1898, they charged up Kettle Hill, which had been held by Spanish soldiers. Although many of Roosevelt's men died doing so, they pushed the Spanish from Kettle Hill. The Rough Riders then crossed a valley and helped capture San Juan Hill. Soon after, Spain surrendered, and many Americans credited the Rough Riders. A peace **treaty** gave Cuba its independence, and the United States took control of the Philippines, Puerto Rico, and Guam, which had formerly been Spanish territories. Roosevelt later said that the day of the battle was the greatest of his life. In the photograph on page 20, Roosevelt (standing to the left of the flag) is shown with the Rough Riders atop San Juan Hill.

roughly one thousand soldiers included many cowboys, Indian scouts, policemen, and athletes Roosevelt had known for years. In June 1898, the Rough Riders landed in Cuba. There the soldiers fought bravely, especially in the Battle of San Juan Hill, where Roosevelt himself led a charge on foot. After the Americans captured the hill, the fighting came close to ending—the peace treaty was signed in August.

Theodore Roosevelt came out of the war a national hero. Crowds came out to meet him when he arrived back in New York. At that time, there was trouble in the government of New York State. The public found out that money that was supposed to be spent on repairs to the Erie Canal was being used by the governor for other things. The Republican Party wanted to replace him with someone the public could trust. They asked Theodore Roosevelt to run for governor.

Roosevelt was so popular that he easily won the election. As governor, he acted as he had as the U.S. civil service commissioner and New York police commissioner—as a tough reformer. His goal was always to clean up the government, eliminating corruption. Other Republicans did not like this because they thought he was too independent. They were used to having a man in office who would watch out for their interests.

In 1900, Theodore Roosevelt ran for office once more. But he did not run for a second term as governor. The Republicans of New York, wanting to get him out of their state politics, had persuaded the leaders of the national party to **nominate** him as their **candidate** for vice president. President William McKinley was running for reelection. His vice president, Garrett Hobart, had died recently and needed to be replaced.

McKinley and Roosevelt easily won the election of 1900. They were **inaugurated** in March 1901. But six months later, McKinley's second term suddenly ended. McKinley was a man who liked to stay in

When President William McKinley ran for a second term in office, Theodore Roosevelt was his vice-presidential running mate.

FOR PRESIDENT

FOR VICE PRESIDENT

WM. McKINLEY.

THEO. ROOSEVELT.

touch with the public and looked for opportunities to go out and talk to Americans. On September 6, he visited the Pan-American Exposition, a fair being held in Buffalo, New York. One of the many people waiting in line to meet him shot him. Eight days later, he died from his wound.

Roosevelt had just finished climbing Mount Marcy, the highest peak in the Adirondacks, when he received news of McKinley's death.

*President McKinley was shot by an **assassin** on September 6, 1901 (right). When McKinley died eight days later, Vice President Theodore Roosevelt suddenly became president.*

CHAPTER FOUR

PRESIDENT ROOSEVELT

When President McKinley died on September 14, 1901, Theodore Roosevelt became president. At age 42, he was the youngest president ever. But he was well prepared. He had already been involved in politics for 20 years. He was a smart man with a fine education. All his life, Roosevelt had loved to read. He kept up to date on the issues of his day and fought hard for what he believed was right. To win support for his many causes, Roosevelt went directly to the American people. In a loud, clear voice, he made many speeches. To get his point across, he pounded his fist on the podium. Newspapers ran many articles about him and his ideas. Americans soon came to love and admire their new president.

Roosevelt was happy as president. "I don't think any president ever enjoyed himself more than I did," he once said.

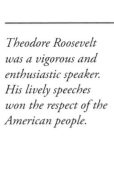

The president's
mansion officially
became known as the
White House during
Roosevelt's term—
although Americans
had been calling the
building by this name
for about ninety years.

Roosevelt was a strong president. He once said,
"I did not **usurp** power." By this he meant that he
did not steal power from other government officials,
such as taking responsibilities away from Congress, for
example. But he used every last bit of power a U.S.
president has. Other presidents waited for Congress
to pass laws before they offered their own opinion
on them. Not Roosevelt. He told the public what he
thought about any laws being considered by Congress.
He also told congressmen what **bills** he wanted
introduced. They often did what Roosevelt wanted.

For years there had been many **strikes** in the
United States. In those days, workers often received
low pay and worked in dangerous conditions.
Roosevelt believed the government should try to

resolve the problems between workers and their bosses. In 1902, the United Mine Workers called a strike. The members of this **labor union** refused to work until mine owners agreed to pay them more money and lower the number of hours they worked each day. The owners refused to meet with the strikers. The mines shut down for months, even though it was very difficult for the workers to live without pay. Their families went without food and clothing.

President Roosevelt realized that Americans were not going to have enough coal to heat their houses unless the strike was settled. He invited workers and mine owners to the White House. He convinced them to let the government help them reach an agreement. The miners went back to work. In the spring, they were given a pay raise and a shorter workday. Earlier presidents had always sided with company owners in strikes. Roosevelt understood both sides. He believed big corporations owned by rich men helped make the

Roosevelt's features were so recognizable that letters addressed only with drawings of him arrived at the White House without delay.

Theodore Roosevelt had six children, one with his first wife and five with his second. Life in the White House was very lively when all those children lived there—especially because they kept a large number of pets, including ponies and parrots.

During the United Mine Workers' strike of 1902, President Roosevelt met with business leaders and mine workers to try to end the strike peacefully.

This political cartoon shows a tiny President Roosevelt ready to take on the "giants" of big business.

United States great. But he also fought for workers' rights. He knew that without good workers, no company could succeed.

Roosevelt also began fighting **trusts** in 1902. The Northern Securities Company was a huge business that owned many smaller companies, including railroads and banks. Its goal was to control all the railroads in one part of the United States. It did not want anyone else to run a train in the area. President Roosevelt called this a trust, and trusts are illegal. He promised the American people he would devote himself to "trust busting." He believed that breaking up these huge companies would help smaller companies. It would also help keep prices lower because there would be more competition.

Roosevelt also made it possible for the Panama Canal to be built. For years, people had dreamed of building this waterway across the narrow strip of land between North and South America. Ships would then be able to travel between the Atlantic and Pacific Oceans much more quickly. They would no longer have to go around the southern tip of South America. A canal had been started earlier but never finished. Roosevelt made arrangements to lease a strip of land from Panama and build the canal.

The United States began work on the canal in 1904. It took thousands of workers to dig it. They

A trip by sea from New York to San Francisco is nearly 8,000 miles (12,875 km) shorter using the Panama Canal. Before the Panama Canal, ships had to travel all the way around South America.

Roosevelt (seated at left) went to Panama to watch workers build the canal. He was the first president to travel outside the United States during his term.

Theodore and Edith Roosevelt had a large and happy family. From left to right are Quentin, President Roosevelt, Theodore III (with glasses), Archie, Alice, Kermit, Mrs. Roosevelt, and Ethel.

In 1902, it was reported that while President Roosevelt was bear hunting, he had spared a young bear's life. Cartoonists began to draw Roosevelt in the company of bears. One shopkeeper asked Roosevelt's permission to display toy bears in a store window with a sign calling them "Teddy's bears." Soon a company began to manufacture many of these stuffed animals, calling them "teddy bears."

faced many dangers, including serious diseases. It was years before they finished, and the first ship did not pass through the canal until 1914.

When Theodore Roosevelt was sworn in as president the first time, he had not been elected; he had stepped in to replace McKinley. When that term neared its end, Roosevelt decided to run for a second term. He badly wanted to be elected president in his own right. His wish came true: he won easily in 1904, by a large number of votes.

In his second term, Roosevelt acted as a **conservationist.** For years, he had loved the West. During his first years as president, he had been able to pay some attention to the nation's wilderness lands. Now he started to put aside more and more lands as national parks and nature preserves. He worked to make sure that beautiful natural areas like the Grand Canyon would be protected.

President Roosevelt also continued to work for reform at home and to strengthen the United States's place in the world. More and more Americans became reformers. Roosevelt devoted time to creating rules and regulations for businesses to follow. He worked with Congress to create laws about how railroads could be run, for example. A government agency named the Interstate Commerce Commission was given the

Theodore Roosevelt was related to both Franklin D. Roosevelt (the nation's 32nd president) and Franklin's wife, Eleanor. Eleanor was the daughter of Theodore's brother Elliot. Her father died when she was young, and she and her Uncle Theodore were very close. Franklin was a distant cousin of both Eleanor and Theodore. When Eleanor and Franklin got married, Theodore Roosevelt walked Eleanor down the aisle.

As this political cartoon shows, President Roosevelt was determined to "clean up" the meatpacking industry. At the time, meatpacking houses were often dirty and unsafe.

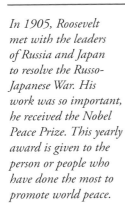

Roosevelt wrote more than three dozen books about everything from naval history to African wildlife.

power to set the prices railroads could charge to carry items across the country.

Thanks to Roosevelt, Congress also passed consumer protection laws. These laws made sure that companies did not produce products that were unsafe. One of these laws was the Pure Food and Drug Act of 1906. It helped ensure that medicines were safe. The law also stated that food had to be labeled to show what ingredients were in it. The Meat Inspection Act sent government inspectors to meatpacking houses to make sure they were clean.

Throughout his presidency, Roosevelt was interested in foreign affairs, the country's dealings with other nations. He wanted the United States to be one

In 1905, Roosevelt met with the leaders of Russia and Japan to resolve the Russo-Japanese War. His work was so important, he received the Nobel Peace Prize. This yearly award is given to the person or people who have done the most to promote world peace.

of the strongest countries in the world. He did not want other countries to interfere with the U.S. or its neighbors. When some European countries wanted to take over islands in the Caribbean, Roosevelt would not let them. He showed that the United States was interested in world affairs when he helped **negotiate** the agreement that ended the Russo-Japanese War. For ending this war between Japan and Russia, Roosevelt received the Nobel Peace Prize in 1906.

The United States was not involved in any war during Roosevelt's presidency. Still, he was determined to strengthen the military. He added many battleships to the navy. Then he sent what he called the Great White Fleet on a worldwide goodwill tour in 1907. It showed

Roosevelt had a saying he liked to use when talking about the United States in relation to other countries. He thought that the United States should "Speak softly and carry a big stick." He meant that although the U.S. should always state what it wanted in a polite manner, it should be prepared to back up its demands with force if necessary. This cartoon shows Roosevelt as a policeman of the world, wielding his "big stick."

Roosevelt (on the left) thought William Howard Taft (right) shared his ideas and plans for the nation. He strongly supported Taft during the 1908 election. He ended up being very disappointed in Taft's presidency, however. Roosevelt decided to challenge him in the 1912 presidential race.

While Roosevelt was **campaigning** for president in 1912, a would-be assassin shot Roosevelt in the chest. Roosevelt did not stop, but continued giving his speech. An eyeglasses case and a roll of papers in his chest pocket saved his life.

other countries around the world how large and powerful the U.S. Navy had become. It was also the first time a national navy force had circled the globe.

In 1904, Roosevelt had promised Americans that he would not run for president in 1908, but he wanted someone who shared many of his ideas to win the election. So he convinced the Republican Party to nominate his secretary of war, William Howard Taft, as its candidate in the presidential election of 1908. Taft won the election. Unfortunately, Roosevelt did not like what Taft did in office. Still, the Republicans nominated Taft as their candidate again for the election of 1912. Roosevelt formed a new **political party,** called the Progressive Party, so he could run for president again. He lost the election.

Roosevelt's health began to fail, but he continued to live a busy life. He went on a safari in Africa and explored the Amazon River of South America. He published his life story, as well as other books. He also turned down the Republican Party's nomination for governor of New York.

In 1914, World War I broke out in Europe. Roosevelt believed that the United States should

The Progressive Party was nicknamed the "Bull Moose Party" after Roosevelt described himself as "fit as a bull moose" during his 1912 campaign for president.

Roosevelt's lifelong interest in hunting and his love of adventure took him to Africa shortly after he left the presidency. Here he is shown (at left) riding a camel in Sudan.

In 1914, Theodore Roosevelt had one last great adventure, when he went to South America to explore its rivers and jungles.

become involved and fight against Germany with Great Britain, France, and Russia. The United States did join the fight, but not until 1917. Unfortunately, Roosevelt's son Quentin, a fighter pilot, died in the war. Sixty-year-old Theodore Roosevelt died in his sleep at home less than six months later, on January 6, 1919.

President Theodore Roosevelt was a popular president who led with great power. Many considered him the most important American of his generation. After his death, Americans still held him in high regard. Roosevelt is one of the four faces carved on South Dakota's Mount Rushmore, a monument to the greatest presidents of all time. He is joined by George Washington, Thomas Jefferson, and Abraham Lincoln. Today Americans still admire Roosevelt for his enthusiasm and for the strength of his character.

Mount Rushmore includes the faces of four of the nation's most respected presidents (from left to right): George Washington, Thomas Jefferson, Theodore Roosevelt, and Abraham Lincoln.

THEODORE ROOSEVELT, CONSERVATIONIST

Theodore Roosevelt loved the American West. As president, he worried that America's wilderness would be exploited, or overused. Mining, logging, farming, ranching, and the building of towns and cities would change the land forever— for the worse, in Roosevelt's opinion. Thus, he became a conservationist, a person dedicated to saving wilderness. He is shown here with John Muir, a well-known American naturalist.

Roosevelt supported an act that helped manage water in the Southwest. He held a conservation conference at the White House. Under his leadership, the U.S. Forest Service set aside 16 million acres of land as national forests. He also created 53 wildlife reserves, 16 national monuments, and five new national parks. He was the first president to make the environment an important issue. "We are not building this country of ours for a day. It is to last through the ages," he declared. Many modern Americans admire Roosevelt for his commitment to protecting the wilderness.

Time Line

1850	1860	1870	1880	1890

1858
Theodore Roosevelt is born on October 27.

1869
The Roosevelt family travels to Europe.

1870
Roosevelt starts lifting weights, hoping to make his body stronger.

1872
Roosevelt's father buys him a gun. Theodore will enjoy hunting for the rest of his life. The same year, the Roosevelt family travels to Egypt.

1876
Roosevelt enrolls at Harvard College in Massachusetts.

1878
Roosevelt's father dies of cancer.

1880
Roosevelt graduates from Harvard in June. That summer, he takes his first trip to the West. On October 27, he marries Alice Lee.

1881
Roosevelt is elected to the New York State Assembly.

1883
Roosevelt takes his second trip to the West and buys land in present-day North Dakota.

1884
Roosevelt's mother and wife die in February within 24 hours of each other. Alice had just given birth to a baby girl, also named Alice. To help ease the terrible pain he feels, Roosevelt again travels to the West, where he establishes two cattle ranches on his land in North Dakota.

1886
Roosevelt marries Edith Carow. He runs for mayor of New York City but loses the election.

1897
Roosevelt is named assistant secretary of the U.S. Navy.

1898
After serving in a number of important government positions, Roosevelt volunteers for the army and fights in the Spanish-American War. His regiment, the Rough Riders, win the Battle of San Juan Hill, the most important battle of the war. He comes home a hero and is elected governor of New York.

1900
Roosevelt wins election as vice president of the United States. William McKinley is president.

1901
Roosevelt becomes president after McKinley dies on September 14.

1902
Roosevelt helps settle the United Mine Workers' strike. He begins fighting trusts and negotiates with Panama to build a canal in that country.

1904
Construction of the Panama Canal begins. Roosevelt is elected to a second term as president.

1906
Thanks to Roosevelt's efforts, Congress passes the Pure Food and Drug Act, which ensures that Americans have safe food and medicine. Roosevelt wins the Nobel Peace Prize after he helps end the Russo-Japanese War.

1907
Roosevelt sends the U.S. Navy on a goodwill tour around the world to display its strength.

1908
William Howard Taft, Roosevelt's secretary of war, is elected the 27th president of the United States.

1909
After his term ends, Roosevelt embarks on an African Safari.

1912
Republicans again choose Taft as their presidential candidate, although Roosevelt campaigns for the nomination. Roosevelt starts the Progressive Party and runs for president once more, but he is not elected. Woodrow Wilson becomes the 28th president.

1913
Roosevelt publishes his autobiography, the story of his life. He sets sail for South America in October.

1914
The first ship travels through the Panama Canal. World War I begins in Europe. Roosevelt believes the United States should become involved.

1919
Theodore Roosevelt dies on January 6 at age 60.

THE WORLDS CONSTABLE.

GLOSSARY

assassin (uh-SASS-in) An assassin is someone who murders someone, especially a well-known person. An assassin killed President William McKinley in 1901.

bills (BILZ) Bills are ideas for new laws that are presented to a group of lawmakers. Roosevelt told Congress what bills he wanted introduced.

bribes (BRYBZ) Bribes are rewards (such as money) given in exchange for doing something dishonest. People in the U.S. Customhouse accepted bribes in exchange for allowing illegal goods into the country.

campaigning (kam-PAYN-ing) Campaigning is doing activities to win an election, such as meeting voters and making speeches. While Roosevelt was campaigning for president in 1912, someone tried to assassinate him.

candidate (KAN-dih-det) A candidate is a person running in an election. Roosevelt was the vice-presidential candidate in 1900.

Confederacy (kuhn-FED-ur-uh-see) The Confederacy was a group of 11 states that declared itself independent of the United states just before the Civil War. Roosevelt's mother had relatives who had fought for the Confederacy during the Civil War.

conservationist (kon-sur-VAY-shun-ist) A conservationist is someone who is concerned with protecting nature, wildlife, and natural resources. Theodore Roosevelt was a conservationist.

corruption (kor-UP-shun) Corruption is when someone engages in dishonest practices. While serving in the New York State assembly, Roosevelt worked to stamp out corruption in New York government.

devastated (DEV-uh-stay-tid) Devastated means shocked or distressed. Roosevelt was devastated by the deaths of his mother and his first wife, Alice.

inaugurated (in-AW-gyuh-rayt-id) When public officials are inaugurated, they are sworn into office. Vice President Roosevelt and President McKinley were inaugurated in March of 1901.

labor union (LAY-bor YOON-yen) A labor union is a group of workers who band together to demand better wages or improved working conditions. The United Mine Workers is a labor union for miners.

legislature (LEJ-ih-slay-chur) A legislature is the part of a government that makes laws. The New York State Assembly is part of the state legislature.

negotiate (nee-GOH-shee-ayt) If people negotiate, they talk things over and try to come to an agreement. Roosevelt helped negotiate an agreement that ended the Russo-Japanese War.

nominate (NOM-ih-nayt) If a group nominates someone, it chooses him or her to run for a political office. Roosevelt convinced the Republicans to nominate William Howard Taft as their presidential candidate in 1908.

philanthropist (fuh-LAN-thruh-pist) A philanthropist is a person who helps others by giving time or money to organizations and charities. Roosevelt's father was a philanthropist.

political party (puh-LIT-ih-kul PAR-tee)
A political party is a group of people who share similar ideas about how to run a government. Roosevelt was first a member of the Republican political party, but later founded the Progressive Party.

politician (pawl-ih-TISH-un) A politician is a person who holds an office in government. Roosevelt was a politician.

politics (PAWL-ih-tiks) Politics refers to the actions and practices of the government. Roosevelt became interested in politics after he attended law school.

recruit (ree-KREWT) If people recruit others, they convince them to join an organization, such as an army. Theodore Roosevelt recruited his own regiment to fight in the Spanish-American War.

reformer (ree-FORM-ur) A reformer is a person who wants to improve the way the government is run. Theodore Roosevelt was a reformer.

regiment (REJ-ih-ment) A regiment is a type of group in the military. Regiments are made up of smaller groups, called battalions. The Rough Riders were a regiment that fought in the Spanish American War.

Republican (re-PUB-lih-kin) A Republican is a member of the Republican Party, one of two major political parties in the United States. Theodore Roosevelt was a member of the Republican Party.

specimens (SPESS-uh-menz) Specimens are samples of things. When Roosevelt was a child, he liked to collect animal specimens.

strenuous (STREN-yoo-uhss) Strenuous means very active or energetic. Roosevelt believed that people should live strenuous lives.

strikes (STRYKS) When workers call strikes, they quit working to force an employer to meet a demand. In 1902, the United Mine Workers called a strike.

term (TERM) A term is the length of time a politician can remain in office. A United States president's term is four years long.

territory (TAYR-ih-tor-ee) A territory is a land or region, especially land that belongs to a government. The Roosevelt boys traveled west to the Dakota Territory in 1880.

treaty (TREE-tee) A treaty is a formal agreement between nations. A peace treaty gave Cuba its independence from Spain after the Spanish-American War.

trusts (TRUSTS) Trusts are groups of businesses that join forces to put their competition out of business and control prices. Trusts are illegal in the United States.

tutors (TOO-turs) Tutors are teachers who give private lessons to students at home. Roosevelt and his siblings were taught by tutors.

usurp (yoo-SURP) If people usurp something, they take something to which they have no right. Theodore Roosevelt once said that although he used all the power granted to him as president, he did not usurp other officials' power.

THE UNITED STATES GOVERNMENT

The United States government is divided into three equal branches: the executive, the legislative, and the judicial. This division helps prevent abuses of power because each branch has to answer to the other two. No one branch can become too powerful.

EXECUTIVE BRANCH

PRESIDENT
VICE PRESIDENT
DEPARTMENTS

The job of the executive branch is to enforce the laws. It is headed by the president, who serves as the spokesperson for the United States around the world. The president signs bills into law and appoints important officials such as federal judges. He or she is also the commander in chief of the U.S. military. The president is assisted by the vice president, who takes over if the president dies or cannot carry out the duties of the office.

The executive branch also includes various departments, each focused on a specific topic. They include the Defense Department, the Justice Department, and the Agriculture Department. The department heads, along with other officials such as the vice president, serve as the president's closest advisers, called the cabinet.

LEGISLATIVE BRANCH

CONGRESS
Senate and
House of Representatives

The job of the legislative branch is to make the laws. It consists of Congress, which is divided into two parts: the Senate and the House of Representatives. The Senate has 100 members, and the House of Representatives has 435 members. Each state has two senators. The number of representatives a state has varies depending on the state's population.

Besides making laws, Congress also passes budgets and enacts taxes. In addition, it is responsible for declaring war, maintaining the military, and regulating trade with other countries.

JUDICIAL BRANCH

SUPREME COURT
COURTS OF APPEALS
DISTRICT COURTS

The job of the judicial branch is to interpret the laws. It consists of the nation's federal courts. Trials are held in district courts. During trials, judges must decide what laws mean and how they apply. Courts of appeals review the decisions made in district courts.

The nation's highest court is the Supreme Court. If someone disagrees with a court of appeals ruling, he or she can ask the Supreme Court to review it. The Supreme Court may refuse. The Supreme Court makes sure that decisions and laws do not violate the Constitution.

CHOOSING
THE PRESIDENT

It may seem odd, but American voters don't elect the president directly. Instead, the president is chosen using what is called the Electoral College.

Each state gets as many votes in the Electoral College as its combined total of senators and representatives in Congress. For example, Iowa has two senators and five representatives, so it gets seven electoral votes. Although the District of Columbia does not have any voting members in Congress, it gets three electoral votes. Usually, the candidate who wins the most votes in any given state receives all of that state's electoral votes.

To become president, a candidate must get more than half of the Electoral College votes. There are a total of 538 votes in the Electoral College, so a candidate needs 270 votes to win. If nobody receives 270 Electoral College votes, the House of Representatives chooses the president.

With the Electoral College system, the person who receives the most votes nationwide does not always receive the most electoral votes. This happened most recently in 2000, when Al Gore received half a million more national votes than George W. Bush. Bush became president because he had more Electoral College votes.

THE WHITE HOUSE

The White House is the official home of the president of the United States. It is located at 1600 Pennsylvania Avenue NW in Washington, D.C. In 1792, a contest was held to select the architect who would design the president's home. James Hoban won. Construction took eight years.

The first president, George Washington, never lived in the White House. The second president, John Adams, moved into the house in 1800, though the inside was not yet complete. During the War of 1812, British soldiers burned down much of the White House. It was rebuilt several years later.

The White House was changed through the years. Porches were added, and President Theodore Roosevelt added the West Wing. President William Taft changed the shape of the presidential office, making it into the famous Oval Office. While Harry Truman was president, the old house was discovered to be structurally weak. All the walls were reinforced with steel, and the rooms were rebuilt.

Today, the White House has 132 rooms (including 35 bathrooms), 28 fireplaces, and 3 elevators. It takes 570 gallons of paint to cover the outside of the six-story building. The White House provides the president with many ways to relax. It includes a putting green, a jogging track, a swimming pool, a tennis court, and beautifully landscaped gardens. The White House also has a movie theater, a billiard room, and a one-lane bowling alley.

PRESIDENTIAL PERKS

The job of president of the United States is challenging. It is probably one of the most stressful jobs in the world. Because of this, presidents are paid well, though not nearly as well as the leaders of large corporations. In 2007, the president earned $400,000 a year. Presidents also receive extra benefits that make the demanding job a little more appealing.

★ **Camp David:** In the 1940s, President Franklin D. Roosevelt chose this heavily wooded spot in the mountains of Maryland to be the presidential retreat, where presidents can relax. Even though it is a retreat, world business is conducted there. Most famously, President Jimmy Carter met with Middle Eastern leaders at Camp David in 1978. The result was a peace agreement between Israel and Egypt.

★ *Air Force One*: The president flies on a jet called *Air Force One*. It is a Boeing 747-200B that has been modified to meet the president's needs.

Air Force One is the size of a large home. It is equipped with a dining room, sleeping quarters, a conference room, and office space. It also has two kitchens that can provide food for up to 50 people.

★ **The Secret Service:** While not the most glamorous of the president's perks, the Secret Service is one of the most important. The Secret Service is a group of highly trained agents who protect the president and the president's family.

★ **The Presidential State Car:** The presidential limousine is a stretch Cadillac DTS.

It has been armored to protect the president in case of attack. Inside the plush car are a foldaway desk, an entertainment center, and a communications console.

★ **The Food:** The White House has five chefs who will make any food the president wants. The White House also has an extensive wine collection.

★ **Retirement:** A former president receives a pension, or retirement pay, of just under $180,000 a year. Former presidents also receive Secret Service protection for the rest of their lives.

F A C T S

QUALIFICATIONS

To run for president, a candidate must

- ★ be at least 35 years old
- ★ be a citizen who was born in the United States
- ★ have lived in the United States for 14 years

TERM OF OFFICE

A president's term of office is four years.
No president can stay in office for more than two terms.

ELECTION DATE

The presidential election takes place every four years on the first Tuesday of November.

INAUGURATION DATE

Presidents are inaugurated on January 20.

OATH OF OFFICE

I do solemnly swear I will faithfully execute the office of the President of the United States and will to the best of my ability preserve, protect, and defend the Constitution of the United States.

WRITE A LETTER TO THE PRESIDENT

One of the best things about being a U.S. citizen is that Americans get to participate in their government. They can speak out if they feel government leaders aren't doing their jobs. They can also praise leaders who are going the extra mile. Do you have something you'd like the president to do? Should the president worry more about the environment and encourage people to recycle? Should the government spend more money on our schools? You can write a letter to the president to say how you feel!

1600 Pennsylvania Avenue
Washington, D.C. 20500
You can even send an e-mail to: president@whitehouse.gov

BOOKS

The editors of *Time for Kids,* with Lisa deMauro. *Theodore Roosevelt: The Adventurous President.* New York: HarperCollins, 2005.

Elish, Dan. *Theodore Roosevelt.* New York: Marshall Cavendish, 2008.

Harness, Cheryl. *The Remarkable, Rough-Riding Life of Theodore Roosevelt and the Rise of Empire America.* Washington, D.C.: National Geographic Children's Books, 2007.

Kraft, Betsy Harvey. *Theodore Roosevelt: Champion of the American Spirit.* New York: Clarion Books, 2003.

Marrin, Albert. *The Great Adventure: Theodore Roosevelt and the Rise of Modern America.* New York: Dutton Children's Books, 2007.

Roosevelt, Theodore. *The Rough Riders.* New York: Library of America, 2004.

VIDEOS

American Experience: TR. VHS (Atlanta: Turner Home Entertainment, 1997).

The American President. DVD, VHS (Alexandria, VA: PBS Home Video, 2000).

The History Channel Presents The Presidents. DVD (New York: A & E Home Video, 2005).

National Geographic's Inside the White House. DVD (Washington, D.C.: National Geographic Video, 2003).

Theodore Roosevelt: Roughrider to Rushmore. VHS (New York: A & E Home Video, 1996).

INTERNET SITES

Visit our Web page for lots of links about Theodore Roosevelt and other U.S. presidents:

http://www.childsworld.com/links

Note to Parents, Teachers, and Librarians: We routinely verify our Web links to make sure they are safe, active sites—so encourage your readers to check them out!

INDEX